BACK OFF! ANIMAL DEFENSES

VENOMOUS ANIMALS

by Cari Meister

pogo

Ideas for Parents and Teachers

Pogo Books let children practice reading informational text while introducing them to nonfiction features such as headings, labels, sidebars, maps, and diagrams, as well as a table of contents, glossary, and index.

Carefully leveled text with a strong photo match offers early fluent readers the support they need to succeed.

Before Reading

- "Walk" through the book and point out the various nonfiction features. Ask the student what purpose each feature serves.
- Look at the glossary together. Read and discuss the words.

Read the Book

- Have the child read the book independently.
- Invite him or her to list questions that arise from reading.

After Reading

- Discuss the child's questions. Talk about how he or she might find answers to those questions.
- Prompt the child to think more. Ask: Have you seen any of the venomous animals mentioned in the book? Can you think of any venomous animals that aren't discussed?

Pogo Books are published by Jump!
5357 Penn Avenue South
Minneapolis, MN 55419
www.jumplibrary.com

Library of Congress Cataloging-in-Publication Data

Meister, Cari, author.
Venomous animals / by Cari Meister.
pages cm. – (Back off! Animal defenses)
Includes bibliographical references and index.
ISBN 978-1-62031-313-8 (hardcover: alk. paper)
ISBN 978-1-62496-379-7 (ebook)
1. Poisonous animals–Juvenile literature.
2. Venom–Juvenile literature.
3. Animal weapons–Juvenile literature.
4. Animal defenses–Juvenile literature. I. Title.
QL100.M45 2016
591.6'5–dc23

2015035220

Series Editor: Jenny Fretland VanVoorst
Series Designer: Anna Peterson
Book Designer: Lindaanne Donohoe
Photo Researcher: Jenny Fretland VanVoorst

Photo Credits: All photos by Shutterstock except: Biosphoto, 6-7, 8-9; Dreamstime, 20-21; Getty, 5; SuperStock, 1, 16-17, 18; Thinkstock, cover.

Printed in the United States of America at Corporate Graphics in North Mankato, Minnesota.

TABLE OF CONTENTS

CHAPTER 1

DEADLY BITES

What do you think of when you think of **venomous** animals? Do you think of snakes? Most people do. Although most snakes are not venomous, some are. And they can be deadly!

The inland taipan is the most poisonous snake. Luckily, it lives way out in the Australian desert!

A cobra is a shy animal—except when it senses danger. Then it becomes fierce. Here comes a **mongoose**. What does she want? Dinner! The mongoose zips around the cobra.

The cobra raises his head. His neck spreads out into a hood. He slithers towards the mongoose. His **fangs** are out. Venom drips. It would only take one bite and the mongoose would be history. The mongoose backs off. She does not want to fight today.

DID YOU KNOW?

Some kinds of cobras can "spit" venom as far as six feet (2.2 meters). They usually aim for the attacker's eyes.

Snakes are not the only animal with a killing bite. The blue-ringed octopus is one of the deadliest creatures in the sea. A bite from a blue-ringed octopus can kill a human in a few minutes.

DID YOU KNOW?

What happens if venom gets into your body? It depends what kind of venom it is and how much got into your body. Here are some things that can happen:

- You can't breathe.
- You can't move.
- Your heart races.
- Your vision gets blurry.
- You vomit.
- You have painful marks.

CHAPTER 2

SMALL BUT POWERFUL

A bee weighs less than a gram. A black bear weighs about 375 pounds (170 kilograms). How can something so small scare away a bear?

Imagine this: A bear smells honey. He finds a hive. He smashes it down.

The hive opens. Bees buzz out. They **swarm** the bear. They sting. They inject venom into his body. It hurts!

The bear wants the honey, but he can't take the stings. He runs away. The bees win!

A mouse runs through the desert. She is looking for food. What's this? A scorpion! The mouse tries to grab the scorpion. The scorpion fights back. His pinchers pinch. His **telson** swings over his head. The telson is the part of the tail that holds venom.

Watch out mouse! The scorpion's sharp stinger is ready! The mouse runs away. She will find something else for dinner.

pinchers

CHAPTER 3

SPINES OF DEATH

What is that? Is it a plant? No, it is an animal. It is a venomous flower urchin! Hard to believe that something so pretty can be so dangerous!

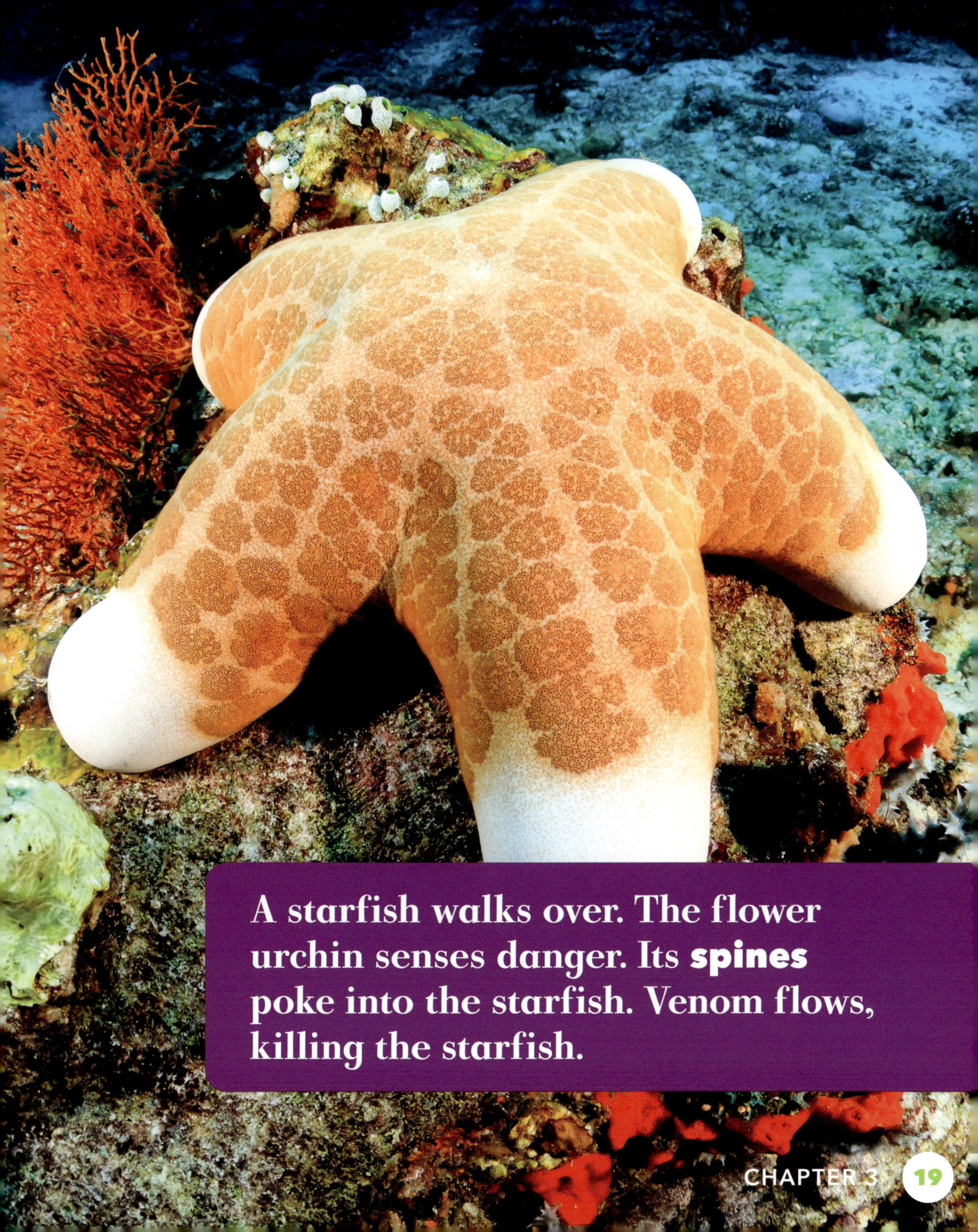

A starfish walks over. The flower urchin senses danger. Its **spines** poke into the starfish. Venom flows, killing the starfish.

spines

Here is an uglier sea creature—the stonefish! He is the most venomous fish in the sea. You would think he wouldn't have any enemies, but he does.

A hungry shark swims by. The shark tries to bite. But the stonefish has spines on his **dorsal fin**. The spines poke the shark. Venom flows. The shark swims away, but the **toxins** are starting to take effect. The shark may live or die. Only time will tell.

ACTIVITIES & TOOLS

TRY THIS!

MAKE A "FLOWER URCHIN"

What you need:

- pushpins
- hot glue gun
- a rubber ball
- a Styrofoam ball
- markers or paint
- access to the Internet

Have an adult help you when using the hot glue gun & when cutting the Styrofoam ball.

Steps:

1. **Cut the Styrofoam ball in half.**
2. **Look up pictures of flower urchins on the Internet.**
3. **Decorate the half ball similar to one of the pictures.**
4. **Decorate the rubber ball like any reef fish.**
5. **Hot glue the push pins so that the head of the pin is on the surface of your flower urchin.**
6. **Using your fish ball, carefully have the flower urchin inject pretend venom into its flesh.**

GLOSSARY

dorsal fin: A fin on a fish's back.

fangs: Sharp, hollow teeth.

mongoose: A small, fast mammal that lives in Africa and Asia.

spines: Stiff, pointed projecting parts on a plant or animal.

swarm: A large number of something grouped together and usually in motion.

telson: The last segment of a scorpion's body.

toxins: Poisons.

venomous: Having a poison that can be passed to a victim usually by biting or stinging.

INDEX

TO LEARN MORE

Learning more is as easy as 1, 2, 3.

1) Go to www.factsurfer.com
2) Enter "venomousanimals" into the search box.
3) Click the "Surf" button to see a list of websites.

With factsurfer, finding more information is just a click away.